SHARK ATTACK!

by Julia March

Editor Rosie Peet
Designer Jon Hall
Senior Editor Emma Grange
Pre-production Producer Rebecca Fallowfield
Producer Louise Daly
Managing Editor Paula Regan
Design Manager Jo Connor
Publisher Julie Ferris
Art Director Lisa Lanzarini
Publishing Director Simon Beecroft

Cover designed by Sam Bartlett

First published in Great Britain in 2017 by
Dorling Kindersley Limited
80 Strand, London WC2R 0RL
A Penguin Random House Company

Page design copyright © 2017 Dorling Kindersley Limited
DK, a Division of Penguin Random House LLC

16 17 18 19 10 9 8 7 6 5 4 3 2 1
001–299082–Sept/17

A CIP catalogue record for this book
is available from the British Library.

ISBN 978-0-2412-8552-7

Printed and bound in China

A WORLD OF IDEAS:
SEE ALL THERE IS TO KNOW

www.dk.com
www.LEGO.com

Contents

Ninjago® City

Welcome to Ninjago® City.
This busy city is home to
thousands of people.

Six brave ninja live in
Ninjago City.
Their job is to defend the
city from dangers of all kinds.

Ninja defenders

An evil villain keeps attacking
the peaceful city.
The people who live here have
to rebuild it again and again.

The ninja want to stop
the villain once and for all.
Next time he comes,
they will be ready.

Lord Garmadon

Meet Lord Garmadon.
He is the evil villain who keeps
destroying Ninjago City.
Garmadon wears a big
helmet with horns.
He has four arms.
Just look at his mean red eyes!

Shark Army

Garmadon plans to invade
Ninjago City again.
This time he will bring his
Shark Army.

His shark soldiers look like
sea creatures.
They are armed with fishy
weapons and vehicles.

Shark-Army vehicles

Here are some of the Shark Army's battle vehicles. If you see them coming... run!

Flying Jelly Sub

Beware of the Jelly Sub's toxic tentacles.

Manta Ray Bomber

Look out!
The Manta Ray is
ready to drop its bombs.

Crab Mech

Avoid the
Crab Mech's
napping claws.

Volcano hideout

Garmadon's hideout is
inside a big, hot volcano.
Garmadon often gets angry
with his generals.
When he does, he fires them
out of the volcano.
This general has been fired.
His clothes are ruined!

Brand-new mech

Garmadon's scientists have built him a Shark Mech. Garmadon cackles with delight. He plans to stomp into the city in the Shark Mech. He will show those ninja who is boss!

Shark Mech

In his Shark Mech, Garmadon can chase his foes anywhere. It can walk under water, on land, and even up walls!

Huge hand can grab enemies

Feet have suction cups to walk up walls

Garmadon sits in this cockpit

Gun fires out live sharks

Mech battle

Here comes Lord Garmadon
with his Shark Army.
He gets a big surprise.
The ninja have mechs too!

The ninja chase the villains
out of Ninjago City.
Good job, ninja!

Quiz

1. How many ninja live in Ninjago City?

2. What do Shark Army soldiers look like?

3. What color are Lord Garmadon's eyes?

4. Who built the Shark Mech?

5. Where is Lord Garmadon's hideout?

Index

Quiz Answers

1. Six 2. Sea creatures 3. Red
4. Garmadon's scientists 5. Inside a volcano

A Note to Parents

THIS BOOK is part of an exciting four-level reading series for children, developing the habit of reading widely for both pleasure and information.

Beautiful illustrations and superb full-colour images combine with engaging, easy-to-read narratives to offer a fresh approach to each subject in the series. Each book is guaranteed to capture a child's interest while developing his or her reading skills, general knowledge and love of reading.

The four levels of reading books are aimed at different reading abilities, enabling you to choose the books that are exactly right for your child:

Level 1: Learning to read
Level 2: Beginning to read
Level 3: Beginning to read alone
Level 4: Reading alone

The "normal" age at which a child begins to read can be anywhere from three to eight years old. Adult participation through the lower levels is very helpful for providing encouragement, discussing storylines, and sounding out unfamiliar words.

No matter which level you select, you can be sure that you are helping your child learn to read, then read to learn!